5 Simple Steps to

MANAGE
YOUR MOOD

5 Simple Steps to

MANAGE YOUR MOOD

A Companion Journal to Help You Understand, Track, and Take Charge of Your Emotion

Jacqui Letran

Dunedin, Florida

Table of Content

Introduction

Congratulations for taking this important step to understand and take charge of your mood!

The first step to making any significant and meaningful change is to become aware of the problems that are causing your negative mood and unhappiness. You can then create clear outcomes to take action on.

This journal was created to help you do just that!

The first section will help you understand your moods by showing you what your current go-to feelings and reactions are.

The second section will help you track, analyze, and take charge of your mood for 21 days. Why 21 days? Research shows it takes 21 days of repetition to develop a new habit - your new and improved go-to feelings and reactions. By completing this section, you will develop a powerful skill to be aware of your emotions and take positive actions for yourself.

The third section will help you use the five simple steps presented in the book to let go of any unwanted emotions.

You deserve to be happy with yourself and to enjoy happy, healthy relationships with others. Let's make it happen!

How to Use This Journal

Before starting the journal, be sure to read the book, *5 Simple Steps to Manage Your Mood.* It is an easy read that you can finish in a few hours.

It is important to read the book first because the journal questions will be more meaningful when you understand the concepts behind them. Your answers will also come faster and flow more easily.

Once you're ready to start, come back to this journal and complete Section One, *Understanding Your Mood.*

Starting the next day, use Section Two, Mood Tracker to create your daily "mood" intention and track your progress.

You can go straight to Section Three, *Taking Charge of Your Mood,* any time you have a disagreement with someone or when you want to release any unwanted emotions. You can use the prompts to work through a disagreement you have had with your friends, family, or even yourself.

As a bonus, the border of each journal page is designed with fun graphics. If you find yourself stressed out, or need to relax, coloring the borders can be very calming and therapeutic. There are even a few blank pages in the back of the book for you to express yourself! Get creative and have fun!

This Journal Belongs to:

Section One: Understanding Your Mood

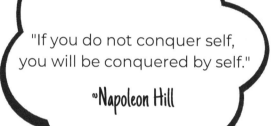

"If you do not conquer self,
you will be conquered by self."

~Napoleon Hill

These are the words I often use to describe my unwanted feelings.

....

....

....

....

....

Of these feelings, I have the hardest time letting go of .... because...

....

....

....

....

....

....

These types of situations often push
me into that mood:

....

....

....

....

....

....

When I get in that mood,
I sometimes also feel...

....

....

....

....

....

When these feelings come up, I typically
react with...

....

....

....

....

....

....

I would much rather respond...

....

....

....

....

What words or phrases can I use to
remind myself to respond the way
I want to?

....

....

....

....

....

....

....

To prevent one emotion from growing too
strong, what other words can I use to describe
my feelings?

....

....

....

....

These things make me smile:

....

....

....

....

....

Here are some ways I can cheer myself up:

....

....

....

....

....

....

**When you have a rough day, come back
to this page. Do a couple of nice things for yourself
and put a smile back on your face.**

Section Two
TRACKING YOUR MOOD

If your happiness
depends on what
somebody else does,
I guess you do
have a problem.

~ Richard Bach

Instructions

Welcome to the 21-day Mood Tracker.

We will focus on chapters one and two from the book, *5 Simple Steps to Manage Your Mood,* in this section. Be sure to review these chapters if you need clarification.

To begin, look at the next four pages to become familiar with the writing prompts.

- For the next 21 days, start each morning by deciding what positive feelings you want to focus on for the day. You can choose to focus on a different feeling each day or focus on one feeling for multiple days.

- Create 3-5 things you can do to achieve your desired feelings. For example, you choose "Happy" as your feeling of choice.

- Here are some examples of steps you might take:
    - Go for a walk.
    - Play with your dog
    - Call your best friend.
    - Bake brownies
    - Finish a project you've been working on.

- Next, think of a few words or phrases you can use to calm yourself and refocus your attention to the positive aspects of your day.The words could be as simple as "Enough," "Change," "Stop," or even words that have special meaning to you. Phrases could be equally simple such as, "Let it go." or "Stay positive."

- As you go through your day, complete your action steps to create your desired feeling. If you get triggered (any negative emotions you don't want to have), use your reminder words or phrases to refocus yourself. You can also go to page 7 and do a couple nice things for yourself.

- In the evenings, review your day and complete the remaining questions. Was today a good day or a challenging day? What made it that way? How did you feel? What could you do to create a better day for yourself?

If you had a terrible day, or encountered a situation you need to resolve, go to section three and work through the prompts.

Remember, even when things aren't going so smoothly, you get to choose *how to* react.

Date ....

Today, I choose to focus on feeling:

....

My top 5 actions to achieve
my desired feeling are:

....

....

....

....

....

If I get upset, I will remind myself
to let it go with the following
words, phrases or actions:

....

....

....

I was able to focus on my chosen feelings:

☐ Most of the time.

☐ About 50% of the time.

☐ Some of the time.

☐ It was a real challenge today.

Today was good because:

....

....

....

....

....

....

....

....

....

12

Today was challenging because:

....

....

....

....

....

....

....

My strongest negative emotion was:

....

Other words I could use to describe
that feeling are:

....

....

....

I felt this way because of:

☐ Unmet expectations

☐ Miscommunication

☐ Thwarted Intentions

I remembered to use my reminders today:

☐ Y   ☐ N

Overall, today was: 🙁 😐 🙂 😊

I could make today even better for me by:

....

....

....

....

....

....

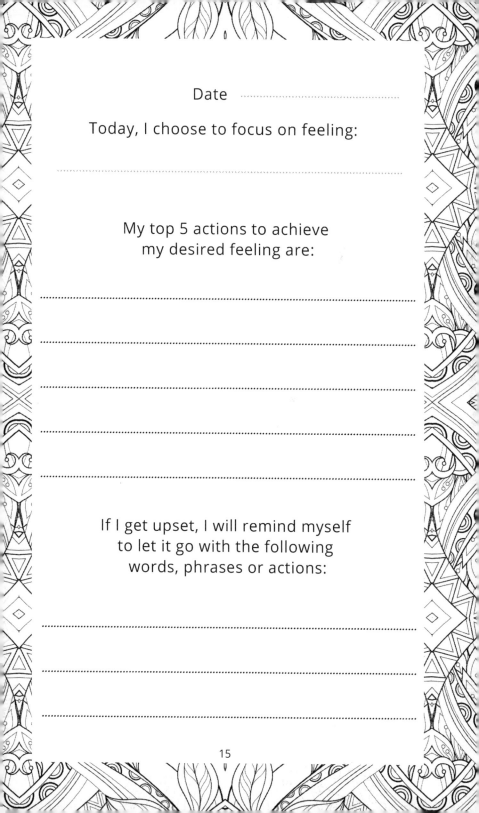

Date ....

Today, I choose to focus on feeling:

....

My top 5 actions to achieve
my desired feeling are:

....

....

....

....

....

If I get upset, I will remind myself
to let it go with the following
words, phrases or actions:

....

....

....

I was able to focus on my chosen feelings:

☐ Most of the time.

☐ About 50% of the time.

☐ Some of the time.

☐ It was a real challenge today.

Today was good because:

....

....

....

....

....

....

....

....

Today was challenging because:

....

....

....

....

....

....

....

My strongest negative emotion was:

....

Other words I could use to describe
that feeling are:

....

....

....

I felt this way because of:

- ☐ Unmet expectations
- ☐ Miscommunication
- ☐ Thwarted Intentions

I remembered to use my reminders today:

☐ Y ☐ N

Overall, today was: ☹ 😐 🙂 😉

I could make today even better for me by:

....

....

....

....

....

....

....

Date ....

Today, I choose to focus on feeling:

....

My top 5 actions to achieve
my desired feeling are:

....

....

....

....

....

If I get upset, I will remind myself
to let it go with the following
words, phrases or actions:

....

....

....

I was able to focus on my chosen feelings:

☐ Most of the time.

☐ About 50% of the time.

☐ Some of the time.

☐ It was a real challenge today.

Today was good because:

....

....

....

....

....

....

....

....

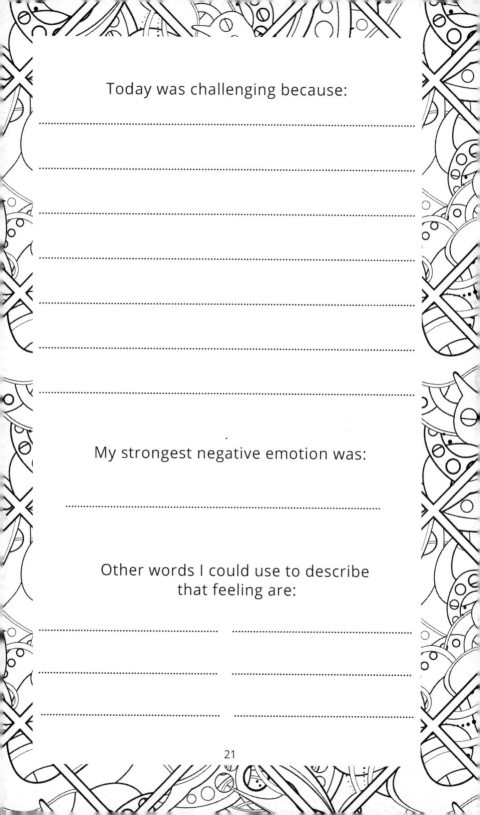

Today was challenging because:

....

....

....

....

....

....

....

My strongest negative emotion was:

....

Other words I could use to describe
that feeling are:

....

....

....

I felt this way because of:

☐ Unmet expectations

☐ Miscommunication

☐ Thwarted Intentions

I remembered to use my reminders today:

☐ Y   ☐ N

Overall, today was: 🙁 😐 🙂 😊

I could make today even better for me by:

....

....

....

....

....

....

....

Date ·······························

Today, I choose to focus on feeling:

···

My top 5 actions to achieve
my desired feeling are:

···

···

···

···

···

If I get upset, I will remind myself
to let it go with the following
words, phrases or actions:

···

···

···

I was able to focus on my chosen feelings:

☐ Most of the time.

☐ About 50% of the time.

☐ Some of the time.

☐ It was a real challenge today.

Today was good because:

....

....

....

....

....

....

....

....

....

Today was challenging because:

....

....

....

....

....

....

....

My strongest negative emotion was:

....

Other words I could use to describe
that feeling are:

....

....

....

I felt this way because of:

☐ Unmet expectations

☐ Miscommunication

☐ Thwarted Intentions

I remembered to use my reminders today:

☐ Y   ☐ N

Overall, today was: ☹ 😐 🙂 😊

I could make today even better for me by:

....

....

....

....

....

....

....

Date ....

Today, I choose to focus on feeling:

....

My top 5 actions to achieve
my desired feeling are:

....

....

....

....

....

If I get upset, I will remind myself
to let it go with the following
words, phrases or actions:

....

....

....

I was able to focus on my chosen feelings:

☐ Most of the time.

☐ About 50% of the time.

☐ Some of the time.

☐ It was a real challenge today.

Today was good because:

....

....

....

....

....

....

....

....

Today was challenging because:

....

....

....

....

....

....

....

My strongest negative emotion was:

....

Other words I could use to describe
that feeling are:

....

....

....

I felt this way because of:

☐ Unmet expectations

☐ Miscommunication

☐ Thwarted Intentions

I remembered to use my reminders today:

☐ Y ☐ N

Overall, today was: ☹ 😐 🙂 😄

I could make today even better for me by:

....

....

....

....

....

....

....

Date ....

Today, I choose to focus on feeling:

....

My top 5 actions to achieve
my desired feeling are:

....

....

....

....

....

If I get upset, I will remind myself
to let it go with the following
words, phrases or actions:

....

....

....

I was able to focus on my chosen feelings:

☐ Most of the time.

☐ About 50% of the time.

☐ Some of the time.

☐ It was a real challenge today.

Today was good because:

....

....

....

....

....

....

....

....

Today was challenging because:

....
....
....
....
....
....
....

My strongest negative emotion was:

....

Other words I could use to describe
that feeling are:

....
....
....

I felt this way because of:

☐ Unmet expectations

☐ Miscommunication

☐ Thwarted Intentions

I remembered to use my reminders today:

☐ Y   ☐ N

Overall, today was: ☹ 😐 🙂 😊

I could make today even better for me by:

....

....

....

....

....

....

Date ....

Today, I choose to focus on feeling:

....

My top 5 actions to achieve
my desired feeling are:

....

....

....

....

....

If I get upset, I will remind myself
to let it go with the following
words, phrases or actions:

....

....

....

I was able to focus on my chosen feelings:

☐ Most of the time.

☐ About 50% of the time.

☐ Some of the time.

☐ It was a real challenge today.

Today was good because:

....

....

....

....

....

....

....

....

....

Today was challenging because:

....

....

....

....

....

....

....

My strongest negative emotion was:

....

Other words I could use to describe
that feeling are:

....

....

....

I felt this way because of:

☐ Unmet expectations

☐ Miscommunication

☐ Thwarted Intentions

I remembered to use my reminders today:

☐ Y   ☐ N

Overall, today was: ☹ 😐 🙂 😊

I could make today even better for me by:

....

....

....

....

....

....

....

Date ....

Today, I choose to focus on feeling:

....

My top 5 actions to achieve
my desired feeling are:

....

....

....

....

....

If I get upset, I will remind myself
to let it go with the following
words, phrases or actions:

....

....

....

I was able to focus on my chosen feelings:

☐ Most of the time.

☐ About 50% of the time.

☐ Some of the time.

☐ It was a real challenge today.

Today was good because:

....

....

....

....

....

....

....

....

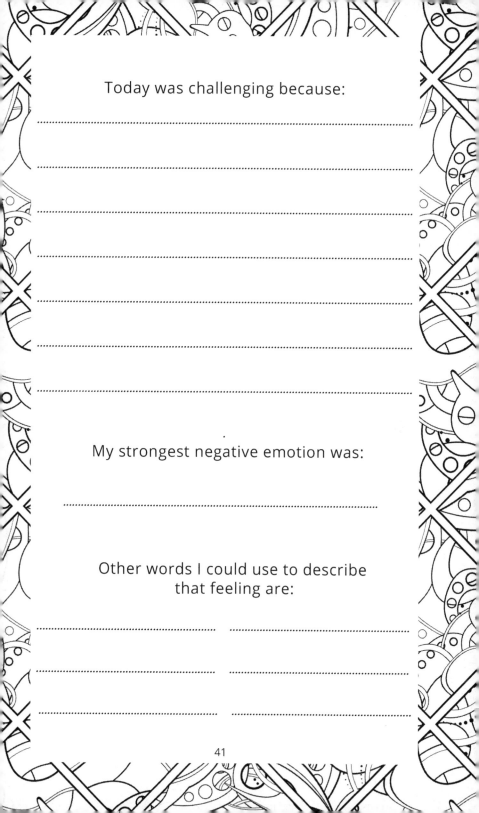

Today was challenging because:

....

....

....

....

....

....

....

My strongest negative emotion was:

....

Other words I could use to describe
that feeling are:

....

....

....

41

I felt this way because of:

☐ Unmet expectations

☐ Miscommunication

☐ Thwarted Intentions

I remembered to use my reminders today:

☐ Y ☐ N

Overall, today was: ☹ 😐 🙂 😊

I could make today even better for me by:

....

....

....

....

....

....

....

Date ....

Today, I choose to focus on feeling:

....

My top 5 actions to achieve
my desired feeling are:

....

....

....

....

....

If I get upset, I will remind myself
to let it go with the following
words, phrases or actions:

....

....

....

I was able to focus on my chosen feelings:

☐ Most of the time.

☐ About 50% of the time.

☐ Some of the time.

☐ It was a real challenge today.

Today was good because:

....

....

....

....

....

....

....

....

Today was challenging because:

....

....

....

....

....

....

My strongest negative emotion was:

....

Other words I could use to describe
that feeling are:

....

....

....

I felt this way because of:

☐ Unmet expectations

☐ Miscommunication

☐ Thwarted Intentions

I remembered to use my reminders today:

☐ Y   ☐ N

Overall, today was: ☹ 😐 🙂 😊

I could make today even better for me by:

....

....

....

....

....

....

Date ·····································

Today, I choose to focus on feeling:

···

My top 5 actions to achieve
my desired feeling are:

···

···

···

···

···

If I get upset, I will remind myself
to let it go with the following
words, phrases or actions:

···

···

···

I was able to focus on my chosen feelings:

☐ Most of the time.

☐ About 50% of the time.

☐ Some of the time.

☐ It was a real challenge today.

Today was good because:

....

....

....

....

....

....

....

....

Today was challenging because:

....

....

....

....

....

....

....

My strongest negative emotion was:

....

Other words I could use to describe
that feeling are:

....

....

....

I felt this way because of:

☐ Unmet expectations

☐ Miscommunication

☐ Thwarted Intentions

I remembered to use my reminders today:

☐ Y   ☐ N

Overall, today was: ☹ 😐 🙂 😊

I could make today even better for me by:

....

....

....

....

....

....

....

....

Date ....

Today, I choose to focus on feeling:

....

My top 5 actions to achieve
my desired feeling are:

....

....

....

....

....

If I get upset, I will remind myself
to let it go with the following
words, phrases or actions:

....

....

....

I was able to focus on my chosen feelings:

☐ Most of the time.

☐ About 50% of the time.

☐ Some of the time.

☐ It was a real challenge today.

Today was good because:

....

....

....

....

....

....

....

....

Today was challenging because:

....

....

....

....

....

....

....

My strongest negative emotion was:

....

Other words I could use to describe
that feeling are:

....

....

....

I felt this way because of:

☐ Unmet expectations

☐ Miscommunication

☐ Thwarted Intentions

I remembered to use my reminders today:

☐ Y   ☐ N

Overall, today was: ☹ 😐 🙂 😉

I could make today even better for me by:

....

....

....

....

....

....

Date ....

Today, I choose to focus on feeling:

....

My top 5 actions to achieve
my desired feeling are:

....

....

....

....

....

If I get upset, I will remind myself
to let it go with the following
words, phrases or actions:

....

....

....

I was able to focus on my chosen feelings:

☐ Most of the time.

☐ About 50% of the time.

☐ Some of the time.

☐ It was a real challenge today.

Today was good because:

....

....

....

....

....

....

....

....

Today was challenging because:

··

··

··

··

··

··

··

My strongest negative emotion was:

··

Other words I could use to describe
that feeling are:

···································   ···································

···································   ···································

···································   ···································

I felt this way because of:

- [ ] Unmet expectations
- [ ] Miscommunication
- [ ] Thwarted Intentions

I remembered to use my reminders today:

[Y] [N]

Overall, today was: ☹ 😐 🙂 😉

I could make today even better for me by:

....

....

....

....

....

....

....

Date ....

Today, I choose to focus on feeling:

....

My top 5 actions to achieve
my desired feeling are:

....

....

....

....

If I get upset, I will remind myself
to let it go with the following
words, phrases or actions:

....

....

....

I was able to focus on my chosen feelings:

☐ Most of the time.

☐ About 50% of the time.

☐ Some of the time.

☐ It was a real challenge today.

Today was good because:

....

....

....

....

....

....

....

....

Today was challenging because:

....

....

....

....

....

....

....

My strongest negative emotion was:

....

Other words I could use to describe
that feeling are:

....

....

....

I felt this way because of:

☐ Unmet expectations

☐ Miscommunication

☐ Thwarted Intentions

I remembered to use my reminders today:

| Y | N |

Overall, today was: ☹ 😐 🙂 😊

I could make today even better for me by:

....

....

....

....

....

....

Date ....

Today, I choose to focus on feeling:

....

My top 5 actions to achieve
my desired feeling are:

....

....

....

....

....

If I get upset, I will remind myself
to let it go with the following
words, phrases or actions:

....

....

....

I was able to focus on my chosen feelings:

☐ Most of the time.

☐ About 50% of the time.

☐ Some of the time.

☐ It was a real challenge today.

Today was good because:

....

....

....

....

....

....

....

....

....

Today was challenging because:

....

....

....

....

....

....

....

My strongest negative emotion was:

....

Other words I could use to describe
that feeling are:

....

....

....

I felt this way because of:

☐ Unmet expectations

☐ Miscommunication

☐ Thwarted Intentions

I remembered to use my reminders today:

☐ Y ☐ N

Overall, today was: ☹ 😐 🙂 😊

I could make today even better for me by:

....

....

....

....

....

....

....

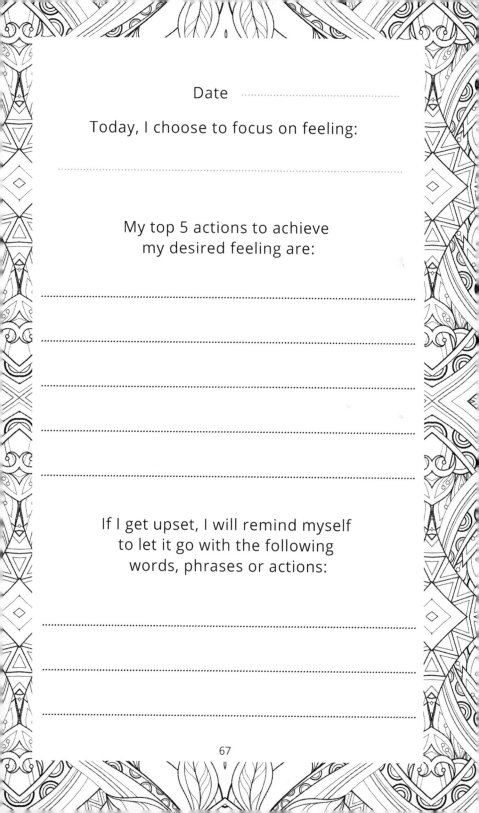

Date ·······························

Today, I choose to focus on feeling:

···

My top 5 actions to achieve
my desired feeling are:

···

···

···

···

···

If I get upset, I will remind myself
to let it go with the following
words, phrases or actions:

···

···

···

67

I was able to focus on my chosen feelings:

☐ Most of the time.

☐ About 50% of the time.

☐ Some of the time.

☐ It was a real challenge today.

Today was good because:

....

....

....

....

....

....

....

....

Today was challenging because:

....

....

....

....

....

....

....

My strongest negative emotion was:

....

Other words I could use to describe
that feeling are:

....

....

....

I felt this way because of:

☐ Unmet expectations

☐ Miscommunication

☐ Thwarted Intentions

I remembered to use my reminders today:

☐ Y ☐ N

Overall, today was: 🙁 😐 🙂 😊

I could make today even better for me by:

....

....

....

....

....

....

Date ....

Today, I choose to focus on feeling:

....

My top 5 actions to achieve
my desired feeling are:

....

....

....

....

....

If I get upset, I will remind myself
to let it go with the following
words, phrases or actions:

....

....

....

I was able to focus on my chosen feelings:

☐ Most of the time.

☐ About 50% of the time.

☐ Some of the time.

☐ It was a real challenge today.

Today was good because:

....

....

....

....

....

....

....

....

Today was challenging because:

....

....

....

....

....

....

My strongest negative emotion was:

....

Other words I could use to describe
that feeling are:

....

....

....

I felt this way because of:

☐ Unmet expectations

☐ Miscommunication

☐ Thwarted Intentions

I remembered to use my reminders today:

☐ Y ☐ N

Overall, today was: ☹ 😐 🙂 😊

I could make today even better for me by:

....

....

....

....

....

....

Date ....

Today, I choose to focus on feeling:

....

My top 5 actions to achieve
my desired feeling are:

....

....

....

....

....

If I get upset, I will remind myself
to let it go with the following
words, phrases or actions:

....

....

....

I was able to focus on my chosen feelings:

- ☐ Most of the time.
- ☐ About 50% of the time.
- ☐ Some of the time.
- ☐ It was a real challenge today.

Today was good because:

....

....

....

....

....

....

....

....

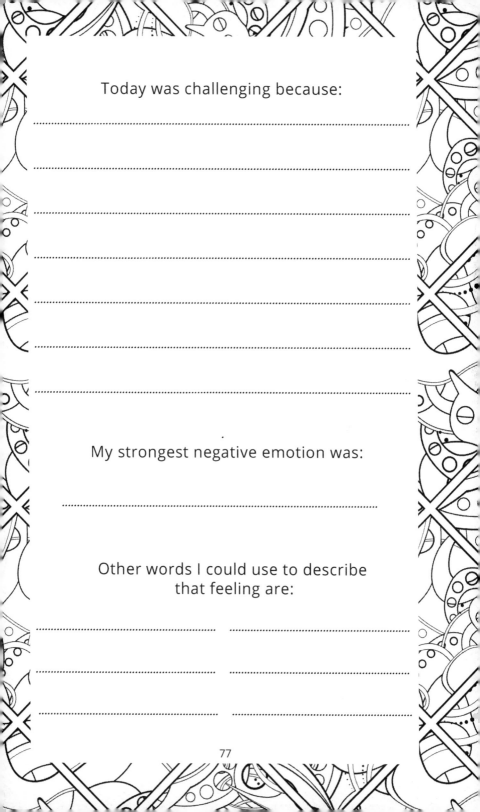

Today was challenging because:

....

....

....

....

....

....

My strongest negative emotion was:

....

Other words I could use to describe
that feeling are:

....

....

....

I felt this way because of:

☐ Unmet expectations

☐ Miscommunication

☐ Thwarted Intentions

I remembered to use my reminders today:

☐ Y   ☐ N

Overall, today was: ☹ 😐 🙂 😊

I could make today even better for me by:

....

....

....

....

....

....

....

Date ·······································

Today, I choose to focus on feeling:

···

My top 5 actions to achieve
my desired feeling are:

···

···

···

···

···

If I get upset, I will remind myself
to let it go with the following
words, phrases or actions:

···

···

···

79

I was able to focus on my chosen feelings:

☐ Most of the time.

☐ About 50% of the time.

☐ Some of the time.

☐ It was a real challenge today.

Today was good because:

....

....

....

....

....

....

....

....

....

Today was challenging because:

....

....

....

....

....

....

....

.

My strongest negative emotion was:

....

Other words I could use to describe
that feeling are:

....

....

....

I felt this way because of:

☐ Unmet expectations

☐ Miscommunication

☐ Thwarted Intentions

I remembered to use my reminders today:

☐ Y   ☐ N

Overall, today was: ☹ 😐 🙂 😊

I could make today even better for me by:

....

....

....

....

....

....

Date ·······························

Today, I choose to focus on feeling:

·····································

My top 5 actions to achieve
my desired feeling are:

·····································

·····································

·····································

·····································

·····································

If I get upset, I will remind myself
to let it go with the following
words, phrases or actions:

·····································

·····································

·····································

I was able to focus on my chosen feelings:

- [ ] Most of the time.
- [ ] About 50% of the time.
- [ ] Some of the time.
- [ ] It was a real challenge today.

Today was good because:

....

....

....

....

....

....

....

....

....

Today was challenging because:

....

....

....

....

....

....

....

My strongest negative emotion was:

....

Other words I could use to describe
that feeling are:

....

....

....

I felt this way because of:

☐ Unmet expectations

☐ Miscommunication

☐ Thwarted Intentions

I remembered to use my reminders today:

☐ Y   ☐ N

Overall, today was: ☹ 😐 🙂 😄

I could make today even better for me by:

....

....

....

....

....

....

Date ....

Today, I choose to focus on feeling:

....

My top 5 actions to achieve
my desired feeling are:

....

....

....

....

....

If I get upset, I will remind myself
to let it go with the following
words, phrases or actions:

....

....

....

I was able to focus on my chosen feelings:

- ☐ Most of the time.
- ☐ About 50% of the time.
- ☐ Some of the time.
- ☐ It was a real challenge today.

Today was good because:

....

....

....

....

....

....

....

....

....

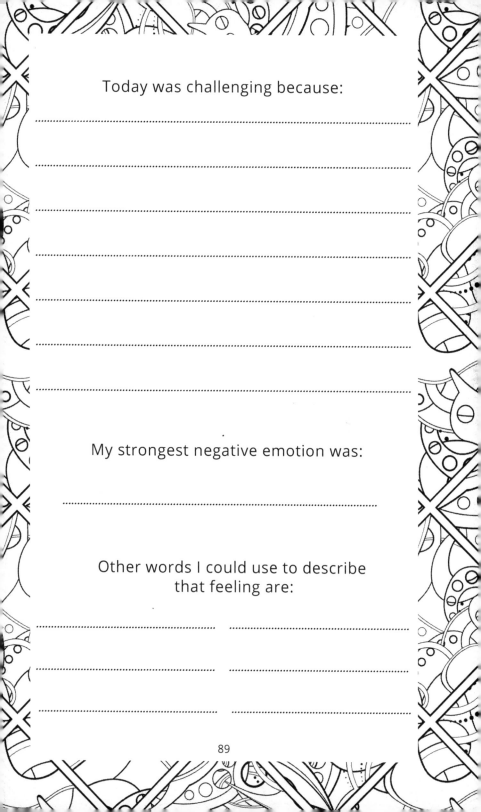

Today was challenging because:

....

....

....

....

....

....

....

My strongest negative emotion was:

....

Other words I could use to describe
that feeling are:

....

....

....

I felt this way because of:

☐   Unmet expectations

☐   Miscommunication

☐   Thwarted Intentions

I remembered to use my reminders today:

☐ Y   ☐ N

Overall, today was: ☹ 😐 🙂 😊

I could make today even better for me by:

....

....

....

....

....

....

Date ....

Today, I choose to focus on feeling:

....

My top 5 actions to achieve
my desired feeling are:

....

....

....

....

....

If I get upset, I will remind myself
to let it go with the following
words, phrases or actions:

....

....

....

91

I was able to focus on my chosen feelings:

- ☐ Most of the time.
- ☐ About 50% of the time.
- ☐ Some of the time.
- ☐ It was a real challenge today.

Today was good because:

....

....

....

....

....

....

....

....

Today was challenging because:

....

....

....

....

....

....

....

My strongest negative emotion was:

....

Other words I could use to describe
that feeling are:

....

....

....

I felt this way because of:

☐ Unmet expectations

☐ Miscommunication

☐ Thwarted Intentions

I remembered to use my reminders today:

☐ Y   ☐ N

Overall, today was: 😞 😐 🙂 😊

I could make today even better for me by:

....

....

....

....

....

....

Section Three
TAKING CHARGE
OF YOUR MOOD

Any person
capable of angering you
becomes your master.

~ Epictetus

INSTRUCTIONS

Let's work on mastering your emotions!

Use this section whenever you have a difficult emotion to release, or a disagreement that you want to work through.

The journal prompts will guide you through all five questions to help you understand and release your unwanted emotions. It will also guide you in creating win-win solutions.

Read through this entire section to familiarize yourself with the questions before starting. Spend time thinking about each question and be thoughtful with your responses. If you get stuck, go back to the corresponding chapters in the book to see some examples.

You will notice all the questions are about how YOU feel and what YOU can do differently rather than how someone else could be different. Focusing on blame or wishing that the other person would change will put you in a powerless position, as you can't control another person.

By focusing on your thoughts, feelings, and actions, you become the master of your emotions. With calmness and clarity, you can focus on what YOU can do to move toward your goals.

Be willing to look at your situations differently with the goal of creating a win-win solution for everyone involved. Get creative with your solutions. Your actions can significantly improve your relationships with others and with yourself.

What happened?

....

....

....

....

....

....

....

....

....

....

....

....

Q1: What am I feeling? (Chapter 2)

....

....

....

Q2. Why do I feel this way? (Chapter 3)

☐ Unmet expectations

☐ Miscommunication

☐ Thwarted Intentiions

☐ All of the above

What were my expectations?

....

....

....

....

Were my expectations realistic
for this situation?

☐ Yes   ☐ No

How can I change my expectations to make it
more realistic for this situation?

....

....

....

....

....

....

....

....

....

What were my intentions?

....

....

....

....

....

Did I communicate my expectations
and intentions clearly?

☐ Yes   ☐ No

How can I communicate more
effectively next time?

....

....

....

....

Did something happen that prevented me from doing what I intended to do?

☐ Yes   ☐ No

How did that contribute to the problem?

....

....

....

....

....

What can I can do to prevent this next time?

....

....

....

....

What were the expectations or intentions of
the other person or people?

....

....

....

....

....

....

....

....

....

Did I accurately understand the
expectations or intentions of the other
person or people?

☐ Yes   ☐ No

What could I have done differently to
understand their expectations
or intentions?

....

....

....

....

....

How might it turn out differently
if I understood their expectations
or intentions?

....

....

....

....

....

Q3. Is this emotion useful for anything?
(Chapter 4)

☐ Yes   ☐ No

If yes, how can I use this emotion to help
me be happy or grow as a person?

....

....

....

....

....

....

....

If this emotion is not useful,
am I willing to let it go?

☐ Yes   ☐ No

Q4. How can I see this differently?
(Chapter 5)

....

....

....

....

....

....

....

....

....

....

....

....

....

What are potential **positive** outcomes
of choosing to be right?

....

....

....

....

....

What are potential **negative** outcomes
of choosing to be right?

....

....

....

....

....

What are potential **positive** outcomes
of choosing to be happy?

....

....

....

....

....

....

What are potential **negative** outcomes
of choosing to be happy?

....

....

....

....

....

....

How can I communicate my goals and expectations clearly to the other person?

....

....

....

....

....

....

What can I do to keep positive as I focus on creating a win-win outcome for everyone involved?

....

....

....

....

....

....

Q5. Would I rather be right or happy?
(Chapter 6)

☐ Yes   ☐ No

What could I be happy with right now,
knowing it's only a first step toward
my ultimate goal?

....

....

....

....

....

....

....

....

....

....

To achieve my goals, what can I choose to **Start** doing? (Chapter 9)

....

....

....

....

....

What can I choose to **Stop** doing?

....

....

....

....

....

....

What can I choose to **Continue** doing?

....

....

....

....

....

Answering all these questions has
helped me realize that I...

....

....

....

....

....

What were the outcomes because of my new attitude and focus on creating a win-win solution?

....

....

....

....

....

What else can I do to achieve my goal?

....

....

....

....

What happened?

....

....

....

....

....

....

....

....

....

....

....

....

Q1: What am I feeling? (Chapter 2)

....

....

....

Q2. Why do I feel this way? (Chapter 3)

☐ Unmet expectations

☐ Miscommunication

☐ Thwarted Intentiions

☐ All of the above

What were my expectations?

....

....

....

....

Were my expectations realistic
for this situation?

☐ Yes   ☐ No

How can I change my expectations to make it
more realistic for this situation?

....

....

....

....

....

....

....

....

....

What were my intentions?

....

....

....

....

Did I communicate my expectations
and intentions clearly?

☐ Yes   ☐ No

How can I communicate more
effectively next time?

....

....

....

Did something happen that prevented me from doing what I intended to do?

☐ Yes   ☐ No

How did that contribute to the problem?

....

....

....

....

....

What can I can do to prevent this next time?

....

....

....

....

What were the expectations or intentions of the other person or people?

....

....

....

....

....

....

....

....

....

Did I accurately understand the expectations or intentions of the other person or people?

☐ Yes   ☐ No

What could I have done differently to
understand their expectations
or intentions?

....

....

....

....

....

How might it turn out differently
if I understood their expectations
or intentions?

....

....

....

....

....

Q3. Is this emotion useful for anything?
(Chapter 4)

☐ Yes   ☐ No

If yes, how can I use this emotion to help
me be happy or grow as a person?

....

....

....

....

....

....

....

If this emotion is not useful,
am I willing to let it go?

☐ Yes   ☐ No

Q4. How can I see this differently?
(Chapter 5)

What are potential **positive** outcomes
of choosing to be right?

....

....

....

....

....

....

What are potential **negative** outcomes
of choosing to be right?

....

....

....

....

....

What are potential **positive** outcomes
of choosing to be happy?

....

....

....

....

....

What are potential **negative** outcomes
of choosing to be happy?

....

....

....

....

....

....

How can I communicate my goals and expectations clearly to the other person?

....

....

....

....

....

....

What can I do to keep positive as I focus on creating a win-win outcome for everyone involved?

....

....

....

....

....

....

Q5. Would I rather be right or happy?
(Chapter 6)

☐ Yes   ☐ No

What could I be happy with right now,
knowing it's only a first step toward
my ultimate goal?

....

....

....

....

....

....

....

....

....

To achieve my goals, what can I choose to **Start** doing? (Chapter 9)

....

....

....

....

....

What can I choose to **Stop** doing?

....

....

....

....

....

....

What can I choose to **Continue** doing?

....

....

....

....

....

....

Answering all these questions has helped me realize that I...

....

....

....

....

....

....

What were the outcomes because of my new
attitude and focus on creating
a win-win solution?

....

....

....

....

....

....

What else can I do to achieve my goal?

....

....

....

....

....

What happened?

....

....

....

....

....

....

....

....

....

....

....

....

Q1: What am I feeling? (Chapter 2)

....

....

....

Q2. Why do I feel this way? (Chapter 3)

☐ Unmet expectations

☐ Miscommunication

☐ Thwarted Intentiions

☐ All of the above

What were my expectations?

....

....

....

....

....

Were my expectations realistic
for this situation?

☐ Yes   ☐ No

How can I change my expectations to make it
more realistic for this situation?

....

....

....

....

....

....

....

....

....

....

What were my intentions?

....

....

....

....

....

Did I communicate my expectations and intentions clearly?

☐ Yes   ☐ No

How can I communicate more effectively next time?

....

....

....

....

Did something happen that prevented me from doing what I intended to do?

☐ Yes   ☐ No

How did that contribute to the problem?

....

....

....

....

What can I can do to prevent this next time?

....

....

....

....

What were the expectations or intentions of the other person or people?

....

....

....

....

....

....

....

....

....

Did I accurately understand the expectations or intentions of the other person or people?

☐ Yes   ☐ No

What could I have done differently to
understand their expectations
or intentions?

....

....

....

....

....

How might it turn out differently
if I understood their expectations
or intentions?

....

....

....

....

....

Q3. Is this emotion useful for anything?
(Chapter 4)

☐ Yes   ☐ No

If yes, how can I use this emotion to help
me be happy or grow as a person?

....

....

....

....

....

....

....

If this emotion is not useful,
am I willing to let it go?

☐ Yes   ☐ No

Q4. How can I see this differently?
(Chapter 5)

- ....
- ....
- ....
- ....
- ....
- ....
- ....
- ....
- ....
- ....
- ....
- ....

What are potential **positive** outcomes
of choosing to be right?

....

....

....

....

....

What are potential **negative** outcomes
of choosing to be right?

....

....

....

....

....

....

What are potential **positive** outcomes
of choosing to be happy?

....

....

....

....

....

What are potential **negative** outcomes
of choosing to be happy?

....

....

....

....

....

How can I communicate my goals and expectations clearly to the other person?

....

....

....

....

....

....

What can I do to keep positive as I focus on creating a win-win outcome for everyone involved?

....

....

....

....

....

Q5. Would I rather be right or happy?
(Chapter 6)

☐ Yes   ☐ No

What could I be happy with right now,
knowing it's only a first step toward
my ultimate goal?

....

....

....

....

....

....

....

....

....

To achieve my goals, what can I choose to **Start** doing? (Chapter 9)

....

....

....

....

....

What can I choose to **Stop** doing?

....

....

....

....

....

....

What can I choose to **Continue** doing?

....

....

....

....

....

....

Answering all these questions has
helped me realize that I...

....

....

....

....

....

....

What were the outcomes because of my new
attitude and focus on creating
a win-win solution?

....

....

....

....

....

....

What else can I do to achieve my goal?

....

....

....

....

....

ABOUT THE AUTHOR

Jacqui Letran is an Award-Winning Author, Nurse Practitioner, and Teen Confidence Expert with over 18 years of experience guiding youth to optimal physical and mental health.

Her multi-award-winning book series, Words of Wisdom for Teens has earned sixteen awards and is regarded as a "must-read" collection of books for teens and young adults struggling with low self-esteem, anxiety or depression.

Through her writing, client sessions, and keynote engagements, Jacqui teaches that success and happiness are achievable by everyone, regardless of current struggles and circumstances. Jacqui is a gifted and energetic leader who dedicates her life's work to help teens create a powerful and resilient mindset to be happy and successful in life.

An avid adventurer, Jacqui spends most of the year exploring the U.S. in her motorhome with her husband, 4 cats, and a dog. When not traveling, Jacqui can be found soaking up the sunshine and smiles in Dunedin, Florida.

Words of Wisdom for Teens Series
Award-Winning Guides for Teen Girls

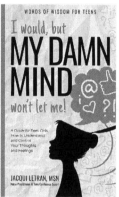

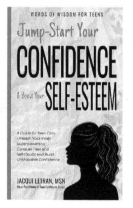

Pre-order Now   Pre-order Now